On Whom the Fire Fell

On Whom the Fire Fell

Testimonies of Holiness Giants

by

LeRoy Brown

Beacon Hill Press of Kansas City
Kansas City, Missouri

First Printing, 1977

ISBN: 0-8341-0472-5

Printed in the
United States of America

Contents

Dedication

to my wife

MARY EV BROWN

A Spiritual Giant

1 / Henry Clay Morrison

Service Call

Little Bud Morrison looked up hopefully as Evangelist James Phillips gave another altar call at Boyd's Creek Meetinghouse in Kentucky.

Will someone ask me tonight? During the past four services Bud had sat near the front, praying someone would personally invite him to the altar. He felt too timid to go otherwise.

Please! But nobody noticed the 12-year-old orphan who had lived with his grandparents and aunt for eight years.

Again, at the end of the Friday morning church service nobody spoke to Bud. And until the conclusion of the revival he remained unnoticed.

The next day, while plowing corn on Grandfather's farm, little Bud, whose name was really Henry Clay Morrison, frowned and yelled at the horses.

Nobody cares. Why should they? I'm only a poor orphan, small for my age. I'll never amount to anything.

As Bud plodded along with the plow, Satan tempted

7

him. "Why don't you really be mean? Bad!" whispered the devil. "Rob a bank or something! Then people will notice you, little man."

Bud cursed bitterly.

But at once the boy's conscience stung him, because on horseback, far across the field, he saw Evangelist Phillips riding with his head bowed in prayer.

Of course the evangelist had not heard Bud curse. But young Morrison knew God had heard, and he felt deeply sorry. He could hardly wait until the next revival to confess his sins.

I'll go forward then whether anybody asks me to or not, Bud promised himself.

Finally revival time came again.

The weight of sin pressed hard on Bud Morrison's conscience. But he was not brave enough to go to the altar until Thursday night. There he prayed long and earnestly but could not feel satisfied.

At the Friday morning meeting Bud became the first seeker. He still did not get through. He tried in vain again on Friday night, Saturday morning, and Saturday night. And on Sunday morning he prayed at the altar during the entire service.

Some of the people had left the church, thinking probably the young seeker would never pray through. But he continued praying and most of the congregation remained.

Finally a strong, elderly man, Emory Hammer, bent over the boy tenderly, pressed his bearded mouth against his ear, and said, "Buddie, God is not mad at you."

"Sir? Sir? Sir?" His heart cried out to hear those comforting words again.

"Buddie, God loves you. He sent His Son to die for you." Then the man quoted John 3:16.

"That's true!" The truth flashed through Henry Clay

Morrison's mind. And he wondered why he hadn't thought of that sooner.

"My burden fell off," he said later when relating the experience. "A joyful sense of forgiveness went through me. I leaped to my feet, praising the Lord. I felt as if I would burst with gracious agony and joy and praise. Mike Smith was sitting on the steps of the old-time pulpit. I hugged Mike, leaped into the pulpit, ran across and shook hands with the choir, and then faced the people and began to exhort them to come to Christ."

Bud's schoolteacher, an agnostic, came forward, hugged Bud, wept and cried to God for mercy. Before that revival ended, he was genuinely saved.

Bud joined the Boyd Creek Church and attended all services regularly. He and Mike Smith also went to prayer meetings at Temple Hill and Old Bethel Church. There they praised God and urged people to give their hearts to Him.

"Something good always happens when Bud Morrison and Mike Smith go to church!" the people said.

Before long young Morrison felt called to preach.

At his grandfather's house he conducted the family altar, and he hoped to do the same when he moved to Perryville to live with his half brother, Tom English. But Tom had little interest in religion. He became angry when Henry Clay declared he intended to preach.

"We don't need another one-horse preacher in the family," growled Tom. "We have one already. That's enough!"

"But God has called me to preach," said Bud.

"Preach!" said Tom, scornfully. "Why do you want to do that when I could get you into West Point? Or you could become a lawyer or a physician."

"God has called me to preach!"

"Well, He must be hard up for material is all I can

9

say," snorted Tom as he turned and walked away.

Lord Jesus, help me! I'm going to preach. I don't care what Tom says. He did start preaching at age 21.

Later he learned that long before Tom had objected to his preaching, someone had highly approved it. His mother walked the floor with her baby son, weeping, laughing, and praising God.

And she said, "Today while I was at church, I gave my little Henry Clay to God to preach the gospel, and I believe that He accepted the gift. When I am dead and gone, this baby boy, grown into manhood, will preach Jesus."

He did preach at various places and held many revivals.

At Vanderbilt University, Dr. Tom Dodd told Morrison about baptizing Laura Dodd Bain, the attractive daughter of Col. George W. Bain, assistant pastor in Lexington. And when the young preacher received and accepted an invitation to visit the Bains, he immediately fell in love with Laura.

Bud tried for more than two years to tell her of his love, but each time his tongue would not reveal his heart. He wrote letters for her but tore them up before putting them in the mail. And even sometimes he went to Lexington without seeing her, because of being bashful.

But finally he proposed marriage, and she accepted him. "The first time you preached at Hill Street," she said, "something in my heart said, 'That's the man for you, Laura Dodd Bain.'"

Henry Clay Morrison always dealt honestly and frankly with people. For instance, at a General Conference, a prominent banker invited him to become pastor of a church in his town.

"But the bishop would have to appoint me," said Morrison.

"Don't worry about that," said the banker. "He will."

10

He did. And at that church Pastor Morrison received twice as much pay as he had anywhere else. But a problem arose.

The banker wanted to tell the pastor how and what to preach. Above all he did not want any humor expressed in the pulpit. And when the pastor said in a sermon, "It's no sin to put too much soda in biscuits, but that shouldn't happen too often," the banker objected.

At the conclusion of that sermon, during a conversation, the banker said, "I asked for you to be sent here, didn't I?"

"I had several other offers at the time," replied the pastor.

"I loaned you money to help you get started here, didn't I?"

"Yes, and I repaid you with interest."

Then the banker hinted that the bishop might be sending the pastor elsewhere.

"I must be a free man before God and the people when I stand up to preach," declared the pastor. "I must preach without any sort of promises to anybody except I will try to discharge my duty with a good conscience."

The banker probably talked with the bishop. At any rate, Pastor Morrison was moved to a church in Frankfort, the state capital.

After pastoring various churches, H. C. Morrison became an evangelist who led many people to Jesus.

He wrote numerous articles and books. Regarding sanctification, he wrote, "Sanctification, as taught and experienced by the early Methodists and by thousands throughout the history of Methodism, does not propose to anyone to seek to be a full-grown Christian by a definite experience sought at an altar. Sanctification does not come by growth. It is a cleansing of a regenerated, believing, consecrated Christian from the carnal mind. St. Paul calls

11

it the 'crucifixion of the old man, that the body of sin may be destroyed, then henceforth we should not serve sin.'"

In one of his books, H. C. Morrison wrote about the unusual conversion of a man called "Uncle Sam," in Frankfort. Sam had been a blacksmith, then a Union soldier in the cavalry, and later a sailor. He could not read or write.

When past 70 years old, he lived in a shantyboat on the Kentucky River, near Frankfort. He earned a living fishing, but spent most of his money for whisky. He swore profusely and fought often. He had spent a term in prison for theft and another term for murder.

He was in jail, charged with wife beating, when Pastor Morrison visited him.

"Mister, I'm an awful sinner," said Sam. "I wondered if anyone would have enough interest in me to come out here and speak a word to me and pray for me."

Sam gave his heart to God, cleaned up, and became sexton in the Methodist church at Frankfort. His wife also became converted.

A few years later, at a brush arbor meeting in a woods south of Frankfort, when Evangelist Morrison returned to that community to hold a revival, Sam was sanctified.

Still later, Sam walked into H. C. Morrison's publishing house in Louisville. "Lost my fishing supplies in a storm," he explained. "I've come to live with you."

"You've come to the right place," said Morrison with a smile.

Sam sent for his wife. A cottage was furnished for them, and Sam became janitor in the *Herald* office. He spent his time working and witnessing, praising God, and being a blessing to many, until he was struck and killed by a streetcar.

Through the years Henry Clay Morrison earnestly preached holiness. And in the evening of life he expressed this desire: "I am wishing that once a year in some central city there could be a conference of the members of all churches who stand for the Wesleyan doctrine of sanctification. We would gather in holy fellowship to preach and witness to the great doctrine of the sanctifying power of Jesus' blood.

"Could we have a gathering of this kind bringing together members of the Methodist church who are true to this Pauline Wesleyan doctrine, the Nazarenes, the Pilgrims, the Free Methodists, the Wesleyan Methodists, and representatives of all churches and people who are not only convinced in their mind, but have experienced in their heart, the sanctifying power of Jesus' blood, it would have a most gracious and powerful effect.

"It would bring about a spirit of brotherly love. It would unite the forces of true full salvation evangelism against the spirit of modern liberalism, and thousands would come to see and remain to pray. No church need be hurt in the least, as all churches, participating in such a meeting, would be blessed, broadened in their fellowship, warmed in their heart, and so the great work of spreading scriptural holiness would be prospered."

H. C. Morrison's unusual speaking ability was widely acclaimed.

Once when he introduced William Jennings Bryan to an audience, Bryan responded, "Morrison, I find where I have made a big mistake. I should have remained at home during my campaigns for President and employed you to go up and down the land to represent me. I should certainly have been elected."

But Henry Clay Morrison's talents were dedicated to serving God. And no amount of money or other influences could have persuaded him to use them otherwise. Surely humanity is richer spiritually because of his dedicated tongue and pen.

Reuben A. Robinson

Uncle Buddie

A country boy in faded overalls and a crumpled hole-in-the-elbow blue shirt sat in the back row at a camp meeting near Lancaster, Tex.

With one eye young Bud Robinson admired a redhead. With the other he took in the situation but carefully avoided the evangelist. He wished he had not promised his Christian mother he would attend the meetings with her.

On the third night, during the altar call, a kind woman went directly to him and told him he needed God. At first he laughed at her. Then conviction gripped him and he felt a strong urge to go forward.

But they'll laugh at me, he thought. I'm so ignorant I can't even read or write. And look at my clothes. They may notice that I have a deck of cards in one pocket and a loaded six-shooter in another.

But this farm boy just had to go forward. And he became truly converted.

After being saved, Bud said, "The people looked like angels. They appeared to be robed in white. It was as light as if it had been at the noon hour of the day, but it was about eleven o'clock at night.

"Well, thank the Lord, I got religion sure enough, and it seemed like religion had got me. After shouting until about midnight, I went down to the ravine and threw my revolver away. I kindled a little chunk fire and burned my deck of cards. Then I crawled under an ox wagon, lay down on the bare ground, and placed my hat on a chunk for a pillow."

The joy of true salvation flooded his soul. He felt rich, though he hadn't a penny in his pocket. He felt as if he would never be sick, sad, or lonely again. Angels kept him company. "It seemed to me that heaven was only three feet away," he testified later.

Although the sandman would not come, Someone Else did. One who had called disciples from lonely seashores and busy city marts bent low beneath an old ox wagon that night and said to an uncouth country boy, "I want you to preach."

Bud saw His beautiful face and the crown of thorns on His brow. He saw the sweat and blood on His face, and the old purple robe over His shoulders.

Bud Robinson heard. And he answered, "I will."

"He was so real to me. I can never forget my first meeting with Jesus," Uncle Bud said often.

He had promised to preach. But how would he start? He asked older people whom he thought had both wisdom and religion. But those he asked either doubted his call or considered themselves wiser than Jesus.

"Forget it, boy. . . . You stutter and lisp so much people couldn't understand you. . . . You have no education, and sometimes you have epileptic fits. Witness, pray, or maybe teach Sunday school, but never try to preach. . . . Surely God wouldn't call one with so little sense."

Poor Bud. But regardless of the discouragement he

15

knew somehow he must preach. "It seemed like all the salvation in the world wouldn't get me to heaven if I didn't preach," he said.

Finally, he tried to talk about his call with a new preacher who had come on the circuit. But while talking, he broke down and cried.

"Brother Bud, I know what your trouble is," said the preacher, kindly. "God has called you to preach and you think perhaps you can't do it. Isn't that your trouble?"

Bud nodded his head.

"Brother Bud, God knows whom He wants to preach; and if God wants you to preach, He will help you do it. This afternoon I will put your name before the church, and we will recommend you to the quarterly conference for license to exhort."

After some opposition because of his unpromising qualifications as a preacher, Reuben A. Robinson received a license from the Methodist Episcopal Church, South, to exhort.

Bud wasted no time using his license. He did not wait for a pastor to call him, but rode his pony across the prairie, and with lisping, stuttering tongue invited ranch people to "c-c-ome to the s-s-choolhouse and hear me p-p-preach."

They grinned and promised to come.

Wearing a homemade cotton coat, a pair of pants to match, and a shirt made of speckled calico (at five cents a yard), the young preacher faced the people.

Frightened stiff, he tried to sing "Amazing Grace," but the voice would not come. He had taught himself to read some from the Bible. So he tried to read from the Sermon on the Mount, but all he could do was stammer and stutter.

Some people grinned, others laughed, and Bud cried. Then God blessed him and he witnessed to his conversion.

16

The people became quiet and serious. God seemed to straighten out Bud's tongue and he exhorted with power.

"Repent of your sins! Get ready to meet God. . . . Believe on the Lord Jesus. . . . Confess and forsake your sins. . . . Make your peace with God. . . ."

Then he gave an altar call. There was no bench but a few people came forward. They knelt near a table. Bud urged them to give their hearts to God. Three did.

So Uncle Buddie Robinson, as he later became known, had preached his first sermon.

During the next 62 years he would preach all over America and travel from coast to coast numberless times! He would cover more than 2 million miles and see more than 100,000 people come to the altar, drawn by the Holy Spirit through his preaching.

God straightened his stammering tongue but left the slight lisp that was a hallmark. His weak lungs were strengthened, and he was cured of his epileptic fits. Yes, God who had called him, sustained His disciple.

Six years after Bud's conversion he heard a sermon on sanctification preached by Dr. W. B. Godbey. Bud knew the good doctor had a deep Christian experience because when people cursed him on the street or hit him with rotten eggs, he continued preaching and praising God as though nothing had happened.

Bud sought and found this same deeper Christian experience. It was in a most unusual place—a cornfield.

Bud was out thinning corn and thought at length about God. Finally he stopped his work to meditate and pray. He put his entire self upon the altar without the slightest reservation. The Lord had asked him, "Do you want *things,* or do you want *Me?*"

"Lord, let everything else go," he prayed.

"Then," said Bud, "I had that strange, peculiar feeling that God was so close to me that my soul trembled

17

in His presence, and it seemed that God kindled up a fire in the very bottom of my heart.

"The only way that I can describe the feeling is that anger boiled up and God skimmed it off, and jealousy boiled up and God skimmed it off, and envy boiled up and God skimmed it off, until it seemed to me that my heart was perfectly empty. I said, 'Lord, there won't be anything left of me.' Then God seemed to say, 'There will not be much left, but what little there is will be clean.'"

During his early ministry Bud Robinson preached and did personal evangelism with the Salvation Army. While serving with this organization in Austin, Tex., he had an unusual and highly rewarding experience.

Stopping at a home to pray, which he frequently did, he found the housewife at her sewing machine while two children played on the floor.

"I have come to pray for you and the little ones," he said.

"Sir," she said, "you cannot pray in this house."

He suggested that she continue sewing while he prayed.

"No, sir, you cannot pray in this house."

"Then will you let me pray out in the yard?"

"No, sir, you cannot pray in that yard."

"Will you let me pray on the sidewalk?"

"You can do as you please about that," she said.

He prayed on the sidewalk. And although he could not be sure, he thought she might be listening.

Next day Uncle Buddie felt the Holy Spirit wanted him to return to that same house and again offer to pray.

He did. And this time she politely permitted him to pray in the house. He also told her about the work of the Salvation Army, and invited her to one of the evening services.

She came and was gloriously converted.

This brought an invitation for Bud and some other Christian workers to come to her home the next day for a chicken dinner. She said that her husband, a railroad conductor, would be home then.

A chicken dinner with all the trimmings! What a treat for men who had lived largely on hard bread and tea without sugar for three weeks.

The husband was very friendly. The first chance he had he also attended church and gave his heart to God.

"Suppose that when the lady would not allow me to pray in her house or yard, I had showed an ugly spirit and hadn't prayed on the sidewalk and gone back the next day," said Uncle Buddie. "We never would have gotten those people saved."

About a year later he became a regular evangelist and was called to various churches in America. While holding a revival in Bennettsville, S.C., he heard about young Baxton McLendon, whom people said was the wildest, wickedest, most desperate and dangerous man in South Carolina.

Baxton certainly looked mean when he finally came to church.

Before the service started, the evangelist walked back to the desperado, put his hand on his shoulder, and said, "Young man, the devil is using you to do dirt." Then he turned and walked away.

For 17 days and nights prayers went up for Baxton McLendon, who seemed to be under strong conviction.

At last the great transformation occurred. The new convert became known as "Cyclone Mac," and he worked harder for God than he ever had for Satan. Uncle Buddie called him "by far the greatest preacher in the Southland."

Bud Robinson wrote 14 books consisting of devotional, inspirational, and humorous material.

He also wrote numerous articles for church periodicals, such as "Bud Robinson's Corner" which appeared in the *Pentecostal Herald* (published by H. C. Morrison) over a period of 10 years.

For more than 20 years Uncle Buddie's "Good Samaritan Chats" were published weekly in the *Herald of Holiness,* official publication for the Church of the Nazarene. The greeting was always "Beloved Samaritans"; the chats were informal, informative, inspiring, and devotional—sometimes with a touch of humor or pathos. The conclusion was "In love, Uncle Buddie"; "In perfect love, Uncle Buddie"; or "In perfect love, and all for Jesus"; with always the signature—Uncle Buddie.

While reading the chats, one feels he is indeed having a lovely visit with a devoted uncle.

Uncle Buddie's last chat was published October 12, 1942, in the *Herald.* In that chat he wrote, among other thoughts, "The greatest thing in the world is perfect love or Christian perfection. . . . The Church of Jesus Christ is the only institution known to God, men, or devils that can offer a peace that passeth understanding. The greatest thing in the world is to know God." Then he quoted John 17:3, "And this is life eternal, that they might know thee the only true God, and Jesus Christ, whom thou hast sent."

In his writing and upon various occasions Uncle Buddie's refreshing sense of humor became evident. For instance, when a woman asked him why his beard was still dark while the hair on his head was so white, he said, "Well, you see, Ma'am, the hair on my head is about 17 years older than my beard."

In Pasadena First Church of the Nazarene, at a golden jubilee service in 1930, Uncle Bud sang in a duet with the song leader, Professor L. C. Messer. At the conclusion of the song, Buddie said he had recently taken up "voice culture" because there were "so many good preachers and so few good singers."

Both a touch of humor and much enthusiasm is evident in his tribute to the Church of the Nazarene: "The Bible is our waybill from earth to Heaven, and Heaven is our eternal home. And right now I want to say, 'Glory to God,' and I feel like throwing my hat in the air and saying, 'Hurrah for us,' for we are the bunch that have the goods. And I want to add, that we have been cleaned up, and cleaned out and filled up and sent out, and charged and surcharged, and wound up, and we have nothing to do but unwind, run down, shine and shout, and the devil can't come around and tell us to cut it out."

Dr. J. B. Chapman characterized Uncle Buddie as being "the best known and best loved Nazarene in the church." If there had been a title "Mr. Nazarene," Reuben A. Robinson would probably have been the most likely candidate for it. But anyone knowing him would also know that he would not want that title, or any title, because he was so honored and happy to be "In perfect love, Uncle Buddie."

Phineas F. Bresee, founder of the Church of the Nazarene, said Bud Robinson was "a marvelous exhibition of what the grace of God can do for a man." Surely the multiplied thousands of people who knew and loved Uncle Buddie would concur.

3 / Amanda Smith

Twice Bought
and Paid For

"Have you ever wished you were white?"

"Only once," said the black evangelist Amanda Smith. "That was when I was the only black person at a church service. I thought if I were white, I would have been brave enough to shout. Other than then, I've been happy God made me black. I've learned never to question His judgment in anything."

Then with a grin she added, "Maybe it's just as well I couldn't choose a color for my skin, because as a child I was quite fond of pea green!"

Amanda was born a slave in Long Green, Md. At 16 years of age she experienced God's saving grace while praying alone in the cellar of her owner's house. He was a Quaker named Robert Mifflin who lived near Columbia, Pa.

Quickened by the Spirit, she sprang to her feet. "All was light. I was new," she said. She hurried up the cellar steps, clapped her hands, and walked up and down the kitchen floor, praising God.

22

Amanda felt so different inside she looked into a mirror to see if the outside had changed. "The change was so real and so thorough," she said, "that I have often said that if I had been as black as ink or as green as grass or as white as snow, I would not have been frightened."

About 12 years later this faithful Christian became completely consecrated to God when she heard Pastor John S. Inskip preach in Green Street Church, New York City.

"You don't need to fix any way to breathe at night, do you?" reasoned the pastor. "And you don't need to fix any way for God to live in you. Get God in you in all His fullness, and He will live in you."

That's it! thought Amanda Smith. God in me! Controlling me!

Then the congregation sang:

> Oh! bear my longing heart to Him,
> Who bled and died for me.
> Whose blood now cleanseth from all sin
> And gives me victory.

Upon hearing that third line, "Whose blood now cleanseth from all sin," Amanda raised high her black hand and exclaimed, "Glory to Jesus!"

It mattered not then that she was the only black person there.

"Amen! Glory to God!" responded John Inskip. And others rejoiced.

Regarding this experience, Amanda Smith said, "When leaving the church, just as I put my foot on the top step, I seemed to feel a hand, the touch of which I cannot describe. It seemed to press me gently on the top of my head, and I felt something part and roll down and cover me like a great cloak! I felt it distinctly; it was done in a moment, and oh, what a mighty peace and power took possession of me!"

23

Telling her husband, Jim, about her thrilling experience could be difficult. Although he had been a choir leader and claimed to be a Christian, he liked to criticize people and thought nobody should become "too religious."

But she sat on his lap, put an arm around his neck, and told him all about her experience. As usual, Jim wanted to argue, but she said, "Now, my dear, you know I can't argue."

"Oh, well," he said, "if you have something you can't talk about, I don't believe in it."

"Well," she said, "I have told you all I can and I cannot argue."

About a year later her husband died. And soon her little son, Will, also died. Then in due time her only daughter, Mazie, got married. So Amanda lived alone.

While attending the Fleet Street Church in Brooklyn, she felt as unusual burden as though God had a special message for her.

Pastor Gould read his text. She sat with her eyes closed, praying silently. After the preacher had spoken for about 10 minutes, she opened her eyes, and just over his head she seemed to see a beautiful star. As she looked at it, it seemed to become a large white tulip. She closed her eyes and saw a large letter *G*, then an *O*.

"Why, that means *go*. What else?"

And a voice distinctly said to her, "Go preach."

There could be no doubt in her mind when, at four o'clock the next morning, she was awakened by the vision of a beautiful white cross. It rested on her forehead and on her breast. It seemed very heavy—to press her down.

"Lord, I know what it is," she said. And these words came to her mind, "If any man will come after me, let him deny himself, and take up his cross, and follow me."

She said, "Lord, help me and I will."

24

Amanda felt definitely that her first place to preach should be at Salem, N.J.

Pastor Cooper, of the A.M.E. church at Salem, could not understand why God would call a woman to preach, and he introduced Amanda Smith in a joking manner. He said, "There is a woman here, Mrs. Amanda Smith, from New York. She says the Lord has sent her." As he spoke, he tossed his head in a way which indicated that he did not really believe it.

"O Lord! Help me. Give me the message," prayed Amanda. The message came: *Have ye received the Holy Ghost since ye believed?* (Acts 19:2).

Courage replaced the woman's timidity, and being blessed by the Holy Spirit, she preached with power. Several people were converted that night.

While Amanda Smith preached in Salem, a revival broke out and spread for 20 miles around. Black and white people were equally blessed. The church became filled with seekers, and services often lasted until two o'clock in the morning. People could not work. Some of the young men hired a wagon to go out into the country 10 miles to bring in a load of people, get them converted, then take them back home.

Some of the young men who were converted became ministers. Other people became faithful Christian laymen.

The revival lasted for two weeks with Amanda Smith preaching day and night. The success caused her to believe humbly that God approved her call.

This was just a beginning. As a preacher and singer she had many calls to churches and camp meetings. But she never went anywhere without being sure God had called her there.

When friends invited her to go to England to preach, she refused to consider the idea seriously. They asked her to pray about it.

25

"Go to England! Amanda Smith, the colored wash-woman, go to England? No, I'm not even going to pray a bit about that. I have to ask the Lord for so many things that I really need, that I'm not going to ask Him for what I don't need—to go to England. It does well enough for swell people to go, not for me."

But after receiving other invitations to go to England, she felt maybe God could use her there. So she prayed about it and became fully convinced she should go.

Being the only black passenger aboard the *Ohio*, Amanda attracted considerable attention from other passengers, most of whom were wealthy.

When some of them learned she was a preacher, they insisted she speak to an audience on the ship on Sunday morning. She agreed, although the only place available for the meeting was the ship's saloon.

"I looked to God for strength, and prayed," she said. "Then I sang 'Jesus of Nazareth Passeth By.'"

She preached from the fourteenth chapter of John and closed the service by having everyone join her in singing the doxology.

Several people thanked her for the spiritual help she brought them.

Upon arriving in England, Amanda Smith preached in various places. She never forgot an exciting experience which she had at St. Helens.

After preaching to a large, attentive audience in Victoria Hall, a frightening experience happened as she left the auditorium. "There was a great crowd that had gathered at the door to see me when I came out," she said. "They almost pulled the clothes off me. It took four policemen to get me into the carriage, and the driver had to cut right and left with his whip to clear the way so we could get started. They let out one of the most unearthly yells I have ever heard. This was all new to me. I had been around a good deal in America and had been to many large meetings where there were thousands, but I had never seen anything like this before."

God also called Amanda to preach and sing in Scotland, France, Africa, Italy, and India.

While in Calcutta she received an unusual request from a prominent theater owner for her to speak in his large auditorium.

"He's not a Christian," friends told her. "He just wants to make fun of you."

"I won't judge him," said Amanda. "I'll pray about it."

She did, and felt God wanted her to speak in that theater. When the time came, the seats were all filled, leaving standing room only.

Bishop J. M. Thoburn told what happened: "She spoke simply and pointedly, alluding to the kindness of the manager who had opened the door of his theater to her. Evidently it made a deep and favorable impression upon the audience. There was no laughing, and no attempt was ever made to ridicule her. As she walked off the stage, the manager said to me, 'If you want the theater again for her, do not fail to let me know. I would do anything for that inspired woman!'"

At another time, after having helped Bishop Taylor hold numerous services in Africa, Amanda Smith was sometimes asked, "What is the religion of Africa?"

To this question she replied, "Well, where I was they had no real form of religion. They were what might be called devil worshipers. They say God is good but that He doesn't do anything for them, so they think there is no need of praying to Him. But they pray and dance and cook large dishes of rice and fish, and set them out at night so the devil can have a good meal. They think if they feed him well and keep on good terms with him, he will give

27

them good crops and good luck, and keep away sickness. If smallpox or any sickness of that kind comes to their town, they say it is because somebody has made the devil mad."

She also referred to a village in Africa where each family built a bonfire outside their door at night. A pipe, filled with tobacco, was placed near each fire in case the devil wanted to smoke! It seemed they would rather please Satan than God.

After receiving much encouragement from friends, Mrs. Smith wrote an extensive autobiography entitled *Amanda Smith's Own Story*. It became a blessing and a tool of salvation for many people.

Among those inspired by the account of Amanda's life was Pandita Ramabai, an agnostic and idol-worshiping language teacher in India. Reading this book brought Pandita to God and into a Christian ministry. And through the influence of this one convert thousands of people in India were saved.

Referring to Amanda Smith, Pandita Ramabai said, "She was delivered from the slavery of man's opinions and from the fear of man which holds so many of my dear people, and a second time from a bondage of sin."

Being freed from both human slavery and spiritual bondage, Amanda Smith said, "I have been bought twice and set free twice!"

She attended school for only three months, but willingly she let the Holy Spirit teach and inspire her. And many people learned from her.

Bishop J. M. Thoburn said, "I learned more of actual value to me as a preacher of Christian truth from Amanda Smith than from any other one person I ever met."

"Amanda Smith preached one Sabbath afternoon as I never heard her preach before, and as I have rarely ever heard anybody preach," said Dr. Phineas F. Bresee, "in strains of holy eloquence and unction, almost equal to Bishop Simpson in the zenith of his power and sacred oratory. The Lord opened heaven on the people in mighty tides of glory."

Always evident in the life of this godly woman was her humble willingness to follow the Holy Spirit's leadings, her love for God and people, and her fervent desire that they turn to God for salvation.

She spent the evening of her life in Chicago, ever serving Jesus, until she went to be with Him forever.

4 / Jarrette Aycock

The Long Way Home

A young bum trudged wearily through the snow along a railroad toward Anywhere, U.S.A.

"Who cares? I don't." Jarrette Aycock had said that to himself many times since running away from home in Oklahoma.

Some people back home would remember him. Perhaps at that moment an old-timer would be squinting an eye, scratching his head thoughtfully, and saying, "Yes, I remember him. And far as I know, young Jarrette's the only black sheep in the Aycock family."

Then another senior citizen would nod his head and say, "He started chewing tobacco when he was near eight, didn't he?"

"Yes. And when there was a fight at school, you could count on young Jarrette being right in the middle of it."

Yet the boy said, "There were times when I wanted to live right."

Would he ever return to his Christian home and

become a useful member of society? People wagged their heads gravely and said, "Not likely."

Dirt and tiredness added years to Jarrette's face. He wore all the clothes he owned. His trousers looked as if an iron had never touched them, and grease spotted his jacket. He wore no overcoat, although about four inches of snow lay on the ground. A ragged hole in the toe of one shoe let snow enter.

Christmas Day.

But this young tramp did not expect anyone in the next town to say, "Merry Christmas, Jarrette Aycock!"

Three times he had asked for food at back doors. He got none. But he knew he must try a fourth, fifth, or even sixth time if necessary. While he had lived without spiritual food since leaving home, there was no way to survive without physical food.

A surprise came at the fourth house.

A tall, slender man with a long, white beard opened the door. A smile came through the beard, and the old man's blue eyes twinkled as he said, "Come on in, son, before you freeze!"

Surprise indeed! This man had looked past the dirt and rags and called him *son*. Jarrette stepped back, not expecting such an unusual welcome.

But the man insisted, "Supper'll be on the table soon. Come in and eat with us."

A lump came to the boy's throat. He swallowed hard, looked down at his shabby clothes, and said, "I—I'm not fit to eat at your table, sir. Just give me a sandwich or something, and I'll be on my way."

"Nonsense, son! Come on in. Mother, set another plate!" The man sounded as if he would not take no for an answer.

Jarrette went in, but he felt out of place in his shabby clothes.

31

The woman who brought the plate reminded him of his Christian mother. It's—it's somewhat like being back home, thought Jarrette. But this kind of life is not for me. I'll get out of here soon as I can.

He heard people talking in another room. Probably friends or relatives there for a Christmas dinner, he thought.

"Please, sir," said Jarrette, "all I want is a sandwich, and I'll be thankful."

"All right, son," said the old man. "We don't want to embarrass you. But if you won't eat with us, you must eat at the first table. Mother, fill his plate!"

Son . . . first table . . . fill his plate! Jarrette blinked his eyes to hold back a hot tear. Rapidly he ate the food, said, "Thanks," and hurried to the door.

"God bless you, son!" And with his handshake the man put some money into the boy's hand.

As Jarrette walked again on the railway, he remembered once sitting at a dining table in a cottage where a Christian mother and her daughter lived. Before they ate that day, the mother prayed, "Lord, bless now this young man. He probably has a praying mother somewhere. So please save him and send him back to her. And Lord, bless my own two boys wherever they are. If they are hungry, may someone give them food. Save them, Lord, and send them back to me."

This prayer had stirred something in the young tramp's heart. But back then he had not yet seen enough of life's seamy side. He must ride more boxcars, walk more miles, and get more handouts.

Months became another year . . . and another. Now Jarrette Aycock lived as a "gentleman" tramp. He worked and had money enough for whisky which he shared with pals on skid row in Los Angeles.

But an unexpected turn in life came for the young man who for so long had tried to believe sin can satisfy. It happened on Main Street in Los Angeles.

As Jarrette walked near the Union Rescue Mission, he heard people singing a hymn. When he stopped for a moment to see where the singing came from, a Christian layman, Charley Alexander, walked up to him and said, "Go on in, young man. You might hear something that would help you."

Having nothing else to do, and being curious, Jarrette agreed to investigate.

As he entered the building, he heard old Jack Fry, who held open the door for him, say quietly, "Amen."

Jarrette could hardly remember when he had been to church before. But that Monday night at the mission he heard Mel Trotter present a message that reached him as no sermon in a church could have done.

Mel said he had been an alcoholic before God saved him at the Pacific Garden Mission in Chicago. Then he explained what a great difference God had made in his life.

When Mel stopped speaking, one man after another testified to personal salvation by telling how Jesus saved them and how their lives had been changed.

While they witnessed, Jarrette thought, That's not for me—not for me. But that night, through an able personal worker, God reached through Jarrette Aycock's stubborn will, and he found himself kneeling at the front.

Jarrette arose from the mission altar with sins forgiven, with new spiritual life. Boxcars became out of style for him, because after that Monday night in the Los Angeles mission he rode first-class all the way through life!

When Jarrette saw Jack Fry again, he asked the old man to explain the meaning of the strange "Amen" spoken at the mission door.

"Well, I saw you on the street the other night," said Jack Fry, "but you were so drunk I knew it wouldn't do any good to talk with you then. So I just bowed my head and prayed, 'Lord, save that boy before he is lost forever.' And when you came to the mission, all there was left for me to do was to say, 'Amen,' because I knew my prayer was being answered."

After his conversion the road was straight and upward for Jarrette Aycock. He returned home. Imagine the joyful reunion with his thankful mother! Through the years she had kept faith that God would save her wayward son. And although at times that faith seemed to be in dark shadows, at last it broke through in glorious reality. Such joy!

At age 25 Jarrette Aycock became a Nazarene evangelist, and for 32 years he served in that capacity. Then from 1942 to 1961 he served as a district superintendent. During those years he encouraged and supervised the building of numerous churches.

In 1951 he launched the Kansas City Rescue Mission where people could be helped as he once received help in a similar mission. This mission is still active.

Being deeply interested in Christian education, Rev. Aycock served for 30 years on the board of trustees at Bethany Nazarene College, and on the board for Nazarene Theological Seminary for 12 years. During several terms he was chairman of the board for each institution.

For many years he sponsored the Aycock Lectures at Bethany Nazarene College. And that college conferred upon him an honorary doctor's degree.

Dr. Aycock also was a member of the first General NYPS Council.

He wrote 15 devotional and instructive books, including *The Crimson Stream, Save Some, The Grand Old Book, The Nightingale of the Psalms, Mother,* and *Drawing the Net.*

In *The Crimson Stream,* Evangelist Aycock wrote, "By the Blood we are redeemed and by the Blood we are cleansed. How often the Scriptures make this clear." To support this truth he referred to several verses of Scripture, one of them being "If we walk in the light, as he is in the light, we have fellowship one with another, and the blood of Jesus Christ his Son cleanseth us from all sin."

In *Save Some,* sanctification is defined: "The sanctification of a believer is a definite work, a great Blood-bought experience of grace. It is a dying out to self and a complete consecration to God on man's part."

Referring to *The Nightingale of the Psalms,* Bud Robinson said, "It is the most beautiful description of the twenty-third psalm I ever read."

This book was translated into Spanish, Japanese, a few African languages, and Braille. More than 200,000 copies were sold.

Shortly after his conversion, Jarrette met Miss Dell Davis, and in due time they were married. She served God faithfully by his side. She also wrote some books—one titled *Listen, Girls,* and two volumes of *Object Sermons.* During the many years she and Jarrette served as partner evangelists, she specialized in presenting object lessons for children. They also collaborated to write religious sheet music and a song book.

When Jarrette could, he visited his mother.

"Son, I'm glad you have come!" she always said. Then hopefully, "When are you going away?"

"Soon."

"I wish you could stay." But in her heart she knew her son must be about his Father's business.

Then came the final visit. She had been ill for some time.

"You are the best mother a boy ever had," Jarrette said.

"Not as—good—as I ought to have been." The voice came weakly.

He wished he could stay longer. But a date on his slate must be filled, and he would have to hurry to arrive in time. A few days later, as he entered a pulpit in Boise, Ida., someone gave him this telegram: *Mother went home at 7:10 tonight.*

Probably her home-going became more glorious because within her heart she knew that someday, when her preacher boy had fulfilled the last date on his slate, there would be another home-going. And a blessed homecoming! One that would last forever.

That other home-going and homecoming happened at 6:30 p.m., on Monday, October 10, 1966. It was another glorious victory on a Monday night, this one over death and the grave. He almost "died with his boots on," because he preached in First Church of the Nazarene at Waco, Tex., on the Sunday night before his passing with a heart attack on Monday.

Less than eight months after Jarrette died, Dell followed him to heaven.

Rev. Aycock preached on various biblical texts, but the Bible itself seemed to be one of his favorite themes. Ardently he defended it.

When preaching about "The Grand Old Book," he said, "I'm not tired of it yet but expect to read it while my sight will permit; and if my vision fails, I pray God will strengthen my hearing that I may listen while it is read to me. I want a copy placed under my pillow when I lie on my last bed of illness; I want someone to read to me from its blessed pages while I breathe my last; I want its promises quoted at my funeral."

And he concluded the sermon with, "In the day of the resurrection I will come forth among the living or out from among the dead riding upon the promise of the Grand Old Book."

In his youth Jarrette Aycock wandered many miles before he returned home. And although he took the long way, he arrived. The former railroad bum became a respected Doctor of Divinity, yet a humble servant of God, a credit to his family, his church, his Saviour. He became a blessing on God's highway of life instead of part of the scum on skid row. It all started on that Monday night in a Christian mission when a sin-weary soul said a heartfelt "Yes" to God.

5 / C. W. Ruth

Truth from Ruth

Reference here is not made to the Book of Ruth, or to Babe Ruth, but to truth from Evangelist C. W. Ruth, whom God called to preach and to write about holiness.

"We have specialists in almost everything else, why not in holiness?" said Ruth, after God had called him to preach that doctrine.

Christian Wismer Ruth, like many other boys, thought more about bicycles, fishing, and baseball than church. He attended church, though, probably because his parents and grandparents were such sincere Christians. And as they had named him Christian, perhaps they expected him to become one.

But the boy's back stiffened at each altar call. He knew if he became converted, he might shout as he had heard others do. He felt he could not endure attracting such attention to himself.

C. W. Ruth received only a meager education in a rural school. At age 16 he became an apprentice to a printer in Quakertown, Pa. Another boy also worked in that printshop. Although a preacher's son, he had not been converted, but he seemed religiously inclined.

The printer himself had good religion, and somehow young Ruth felt religion might be just around the corner for him. He especially felt this when his co-worker said, "I'm going to the meeting tonight."

If he does, he'll be converted and I'll be next, thought Ruth.

His prediction came true.

"At the shop on Monday morning, just one look at him told me what had happened," said C. W.

On Friday night the two boys attended a prayer meeting together, then they went to church on Sunday morning. On Sunday night it happened—another conversion. And the boy who declared he never would— shouted! And he did it easily without worrying about what other people thought.

"The burden of my guilt was rolled away," said the new convert. "The light of heaven broke into my soul; the Spirit witnessed with my spirit that I was pardoned and accepted of God, and was indeed a new creature in Christ."

He united with the Methodist church and was a faithful member. Daily he carried two New Testaments with him, one printed in English, the other in German. He read fluently from each.

Although a year had passed since his conversion, young Ruth still felt hindered by fear, temper, inability to forgive or love enemies, and other negative attitudes.

After seeking for days for a deeper Christian experience, he received it one evening when walking to church. Standing on the sidewalk, he looked up and said, "I believe that the blood of Jesus cleanseth my heart from all sin now." The Holy Spirit came upon him with complete assurance.

"Oh, the blessedness of that hour!" said Ruth. "Surely heaven could be no better."

At age 19 he went to work in a printshop at Indianapolis. While working there, he felt called to preach. But not feeling personally qualified, for three months he delayed saying yes to the call. However, he prayed much about it, and God gave him special encouragement through Luke 21:15: "For I will give you a mouth and wisdom, which all your adversaries shall not be able to gainsay nor resist."

The first text upon which he preached was Matt. 11:28-30. Five people responded to the altar call. Three were converted. This was the same number of people who were converted at the first altar call Bud Robinson made. And how thrilled those two crusaders for God were to go on evangelistic tours together, as they frequently did.

In *My Life Story,* Bud Robinson wrote, "I believe we have never had a finer leader in the holiness movement than Brother C. W. Ruth. He can plan and hold more holiness conventions than any man in the great holiness movement and have the best revivals in these great conventions. I have worked with almost all the holiness boys in the United States, and no man ever yoked up with a truer yokefellow than Brother C. W. Ruth."

For about two years Ruth served as associate pastor with Dr. Bresee in Los Angeles. "Never a week passed there without souls being at our altars," said Ruth. He also founded the First Church of the Nazarene in Indianapolis. Later he became an evangelist.

Although Evangelist Ruth preached and wrote on subjects other than holiness, there can be no doubt that he emphasized obtaining and keeping entire sanctification far more than any other theme. He wrote several books and many articles on his favorite subject. Over a period of years, his articles were frequently published in the *Herald of Holiness.*

C. W. Ruth stated seven reasons why people should be holy in this world:

1. Heaven is a holy place.
2. Because Jesus died to make us holy
3. To live a holy life and thus set the right example for others
4. As a preparation and fitness for service
5. We need holy hearts, lest we limit the efficiency and saving power of Jesus' blood.
6. A holy heart is essential to the maintenance of a clear, justified experience.
7. A holy heart in this world is necessary in order to have holiness when the Lord may return, or when we die.

In his book *Entire Sanctification,* Ruth states three points which, he says, "when clearly and fully determined, will invariably bring the diligent seeker into the experience of entire sanctification." They are:

First, There should be the positive assurance or witness of the Spirit to a present acceptance with God. If there is any doubt concerning this point—any questioning as to the pardon of all past sins—this should be fully settled first.

Second. The second step toward entire sanctification is entire consecration—a complete and unconditional abandonment of yourself and your all to God. Usually there are three stages or steps before consecration is completed: (1) "I desire to consecrate"; (2) "I am trying to consecrate"; (3) "I do want to give up all for Jesus."

Third. When the foregoing steps have been taken—so that there is no lingering doubt regarding those points—it only remains for the seeker to exercise a little faith. We may encourage our faith by determining the following three points: (1) God is *able* to sanctify me wholly; (2) God is *willing* to sanctify me wholly; (3) God is *ready* to sanctify me wholly. If God is now able, willing, and ready to sanctify me wholly, and I am willing and ready to be sanctified wholly, what is to hinder?

"Now there is nothing more to do," reasoned the evangelist, "but rest on the promises, and believe that the blood of Jesus now cleanseth *me* from all sin, because Jesus says so, and praise Him for the cleansing."

Writing for the February 10, 1932, issue of the *Herald of Holiness,* Evangelist Ruth stated, "It is just as essential that people should be taught how to maintain and retain the experience as that they should know how to explain and obtain the same."

Regarding this, he quoted M. L. Haney, an early Methodist preacher of sanctification: "Real consecration includes ALL of life, and is not simply an act, but a life attitude."

A great help, in fact a necessity for retaining sanctification, according to Ruth and others, is frequent witnessing, by word of mouth, to its reality in one's daily life.

C. W. Ruth believed that the Church of the Nazarene has been ordained by God to promote holiness, as evident in an article in the *Herald* when he explained: "God did not raise up the Church of the Nazarene because there was a lack of churches in this country, but because there is a lack of soul-winning evangelism, and especially is this true in the matter of holiness evangelism, which is the distinctive doctrine and specialty of the Church of the Nazarene."

In still another article he emphasized that if Jesus, who was always sinless and holy, had need of the anointing of God to fit Him for holy service, how certainly does the ministry of today need this anointing.

For more than a half century C. W. Ruth preached and taught holiness. He became widely recognized as an authority on that subject. Furthermore, the presence of the Holy Spirit was evident in his Christlike spirit, cheerful countenance, and holy living.

When past age 75, he and his wife were visiting Asbury College. They sensed a transition was near.

On May 25, 1941, Pastor Z. T. Johnson visited them at Asbury.

"I'm 75½ years old," said C. W. "I hoped I might stay longer to teach holiness. I believe the Blood avails for me. And I know of no better place than the campus of Asbury College from which to go to heaven."

Pastor Johnson prayed that God would bless him and make him perfectly secure in His will.

"Amen and amen—wholly in His will," responded the evangelist.

Then his wife prayed.

God's servant, marked for heaven, rejoiced as he said, "The blood of Jesus avails for me, Brother Johnson. I love you, I love you, I love you."

He died at 5 a.m. on Tuesday, May 27, 1941. He had completed the special service to which God had called him.

6

John T. Hatfield

The Hoosier Evangelist

"John, here's a hat I made for you." The schoolgirl giggled as she held out the hat.

With a big grin, John Hatfield grabbed the hat. Then with both hands he pulled it down tightly upon his head and made a funny face—which he was famous for.

But young John made a different kind of face when he tried to remove the hat. Being lined with burdock burrs, it stuck like Elmer's glue to the boy's thick, black hair!

The teacher had to give John a funny haircut to remove that hat.

Sometimes, looking for what he called fun, John acted recklessly. For instance, near Charlottesville, Ind., he stood in the middle of a railroad track watching an approaching freight train. Laughing while the engine whistle shrieked, he waited until almost the last moment before jumping to safety. And a few days later he did it again!

He also tried to trip a steel trap with his nose. But his nose got caught, and he screamed for his father's help. "I never tried that again," declared Hatfield. But usually he seemed to be looking for something exciting to do.

John Hatfield attended school with James Whitcomb Riley, who became famous as the Hoosier Poet. When he and John were boys, they swam together in "the old swimmin' hole." And they marched together as "soldiers" beating toy drums during the Civil War.

At that time, young Hatfield did not know that someday he would become well known as the Hoosier Evangelist. It all started when, at age 21, he became thoroughly converted at an old-fashioned Methodist revival meeting.

"I claimed the promise," he said, "and the light of heaven flashed instantly in upon my soul. The burden rolled away, new life sprang up within, and angels struck their golden harps and broke forth with rejoicing. The heavenly melodies burst upon my soul, and I was as light and free and happy as a bird in springtime. I sprang to my feet fairly submerged in the billows of glory that swept my newborn soul."

The next day John went to work as usual clerking in his uncle's general store. The blessing bubbled in his heart so eagerly he could not help expressing it.

As an elderly woman looked at some dry goods, John suddenly threw the yardstick aside, walked back and forth in the aisle behind the counter, clapped his hands, and shouted, "Glory to God! Praise the Lord! Hallelujah!"

The old woman's eyes and mouth popped open in blank surprise. Uncle hurried back to the counter to find out what was going on. When John refused to check the demonstrations, his uncle fired him. So he returned to his father's farm.

John joined a Methodist church, taught Sunday school, and soon became a class leader. He also taught singing. "There was no music in me," he said, "but God

45

put a new song in my heart, and I began to try to sing at once."

Feeling called to preach, John Hatfield became a pastor, then an evangelist.

Eight years after his conversion he was sanctified at a holiness camp meeting in Hartford City, Ind.

"I felt the need of a clean heart," he said. "Before, I had been praying myself up into blessings without exercising any faith; but when I reached the place where I said, *Lord, I do believe,* instantly the fire fell, and I knew the work was done. The 'Old Man' was killed and I have never seen him since."

John Hatfield witnessed to the indwelling of the Holy Spirit at every opportunity. When he was saved, he quit tobacco, which he had used excessively, and resigned from the lodge. But the most noticeable change in him now was the disappearance of his hair-trigger temper. Never again did he kick a cow or break a milking stool over her back. Or tear feathers from a stubborn setting hen. Even his wife's habit of having to hurry to get started for church on time ceased irritating him.

Of course, after his "perfect love" experience, the Hoosier Evangelist became more eager than ever before to win people for Jesus.

A cowboy in Kansas offered a special challenge. Hatfield knew this young man liked to hunt coyotes. So the evangelist arranged to go hunting with him. On horseback, and with some big greyhounds, they started the hunt.

All went well until the dogs spotted a coyote, and the chase was on. John, who was not a proficient rider, hung on for dear life as the horses dashed after the dogs. The cowboy was so excited he did not notice the evangelist's lack of riding skill. And Hatfield, liking action, really enjoyed the event despite his discomfort.

As they rode about 30 miles, next day the preacher's legs were so sore he could not even cross them. But he had won the goodwill of the cowboy and soon won him for Jesus. The man's earnest testimony at church the night he was saved led others to Jesus.

The way was not always smooth for the Hoosier Evangelist. Once some boys brought an intoxicated man to church and threw him in through the front door as the evangelist preached.

An angry atheist once dragged him through snow. And once while he preached, a man entered the church with a gun, threatening his life.

But John Hatfield feared no man. When facing danger, he said, "Bless God! I unsheathed my Jerusalem blade, turned up my ram's horn, sounded the alarm of battle, and waded in."

Hatfield always followed the Holy Spirit's leadings. For instance, near the conclusion of a sermon one night, he received a note from a man asking for prayer "when you go home." But the man would not come to the altar.

As the evangelist was leaving the church, the man met him in the aisle and asked him personally if he would pray for him.

"Yes, I will," he promised. But before John Hatfield reached the door, he clearly heard the Holy Spirit say, "You must pray with that man before he leaves the church tonight."

The man did not readily respond when urged to kneel for prayer, but finally he did. He found the spiritual victory he sought.

At two o'clock the very next morning, this man, while working as a railroad brakeman, missed his footing and fell under the car wheels. Both legs were severed and the loss of blood caused his death.

He died victoriously, though, because John Hatfield

had quickly followed the Holy Spirit's leading. The brakeman's last words were "How glad I am that I settled it last night."

Once while travelling on a crowded train, the evangelist felt led to talk salvation to a young lady who happened to sit beside him. She seemed burdened with care. Hatfield quoted her scriptures which promised peace. Then they prayed. As the passenger train sped across the prairie, another heart linked its future with God.

But John Hatfield's personal evangelism attempts were not always successful. For instance, once when en route by train to Los Angeles, he struck up a conversation with a woman passenger. He asked if she belonged to a church.

"Have you ever been in California before?" she replied, ignoring his query.

"Yes, I have. Have you ever been a Christian?" he countered.

"Without doubt, this is one of the most beautiful states in America," said the woman.

"Have you ever made any pretensions to the Christian religion?"

"This is a land of flowers; the air is laden with sweet odors, and eucalyptus and pepper trees are green the year around. You will be delighted."

"This certainly is a beautiful country, but have you thought about the welfare of your soul?"

"When you get farther south, you will come to the fruit ranches, the oranges, lemons, olives, and the fruitful vineyards."

About then the train whistled for a station, and the woman left the coach. But as she left, she smiled and said, "I'm very glad to have met you."

Even the Hoosier Evangelist could not win them all.

For more than 50 years this man fearlessly preached

the gospel as God revealed it to him. He pulled no punches and always followed the Holy Spirit's leadings. He believed in vibrant, active Christianity.

"Some churches are like broken-down aristocracy," he said, "living upon the faded splendors of the past, camping at little Ai and talking about their big Jericho. They remind me of the withered flowers of a last month's funeral; dry, very dry, as dry as Thompson's colt that swam the Mississippi River to get a drink."

He also said, "Some people are like Lot's wife, they back out and crystallize into a pillar of salt. God wants His people to be the salt of the earth, but He doesn't want it put up that way."

A fellow evangelist, Uncle Bud Robinson, called John Hatfield "a cyclone of grace turned loose on the hills of the earth to do just as the blessed Holy Ghost suggests to him."

Hatfield's spiritual enthusiasm is evident in an article which he wrote for the February 6, 1929, issue of the *Herald of Holiness*. In this article, "Seekers—Getters," he told how he celebrated Christmas Day, 1928. He was 77 at the time. "On last Christmas Day we had one of the happy days in our life. We were so blessed that we jumped, we ran, we danced, we cried, we sang, we laughed, and we don't know what all we did or didn't do, but there was one thing sure, we were on the bandwagon that Christmas Day! It seemed to us that everything within was vibrating with holy unction, and we are still having some spells occasionally."

At 77!

The veteran evangelist wrote another article, probably his last, for the *Herald,* November 6, 1929. It contained these thoughts: "The way to keep the Old Man out is to keep filled with the Spirit. Every day we should have a fresh anointing. . . . A violin will get out of tune playing

'Nearer, My God, to Thee,' likewise a holiness preacher will leak out preaching holiness if he doesn't keep being refilled by the Spirit. An empty Christian talks out of his head, but a Spirit-filled Christian talks out of his heart. The Holy Spirit does not live in our brains but in our heart. A head religion will talk anything, but a heart religion talks Jesus and the Holy Spirit."

"To know John Hatfield is to love him," said his friends.

Surely many people did know and love the Hoosier Evangelist who dared to serve within the complete will of God and to point people to His saving, sanctifying, and sustaining grace.

Man of Destiny

"Ouch! Oh-h-o-o-h!" cried two-year-old Phineas Bresee.

The red flannel dress he wore had touched the red-hot stove in the living room and caught fire!

Mother hurried to help. With a blanket she quickly smothered the fire. The boy felt as if 100 bees had stung his leg, but it felt much better after Mother rubbed cool cream on it. Fortunately the burn soon healed, but little Phineas had learned to keep away from that stove.

At age one, while moving with his parents in a big sleigh, he had survived a runaway. Could God have had special plans for this child?

About 60 years later, in 1900, Pastor Phineas F. Bresee survived a horrible streetcar-carriage accident in the suburbs of Los Angeles. Some relatives and friends were accompanying him to various homes after an evening prayer meeting at the Church of the Nazarene. His daughter-in-law, Mrs. Ada Bresee, and Mrs. Mary J.

Willard, a friend of the family and a devout Nazarene, were among them.

At a crossing the grinding of steel wheels could not stop the speeding streetcar which bore down on them. The car struck the carriage, hurling it, the horses and the people, in various directions for about 50 feet.

Mary Willard died almost instantly. All others were injured, but Pastor Bresee most seriously.

Having regained consciousness after three days, he discovered his black hair had turned white. A look into the mirror also told him his face had aged at least 10 years in three days. Although weaker in body, his spirit did not falter. He would live for 15 more years to serve his God, his Saviour, and the church, all of which he loved so well.

Dr. Bresee's Christian parents were not too generous with given names. Other than the family name they gave him only one, although at that, an unusual one—Phineas. Wanting an additional name, with his parents' permission he simply adopted the name of the New York village in which he was born—Franklin. Surely an appropriate middle name. If the town had been Podunk, probably Phineas would not have chosen it, even though he did have a fine sense of humor.

Ever since he could remember (and he had a most unusual memory), Phineas Bresee wanted to preach. However, he was not converted until age 18, at a church in Iowa. It happened during a Methodist class meeting after a Sunday morning service in February, 1856.

"My soul was filled with great intensity for doing the work of the Lord, and I began to hold prayer meetings, talk to and exhort the people, and do all I could to push along the work," said the new convert.

Soon after his conversion Pastor Smith got him a license to exhort in Methodist churches. But at first he felt too timid to do it.

Finally the young preacher delivered his first prepared sermon. He said he put everything he knew into it, rambling through almost the entire Old and New Testaments for about 20 minutes. He wondered how on earth anyone could preach a series of sermons.

That first sermon was certainly a far cry from the excellent, well-prepared, unctionized sermons he was to preach in later years.

Phineas F. Bresee served numerous hardscrabble Methodist circuits in Iowa. A dollar a day was considered big pay for pastors in those days. Of course, he and his wife, Marie, were not serving for money, although ultimately they did have four sons and two daughters to support.

When preaching in a revival at Chariton, Ia., with the temperature 20 below zero, the fire of God fell upon the evangelist. Responding to his own altar call, he laid himself before the Lord, asking for the cleansing of heart he had craved. God answered his plea, filling him with the Holy Spirit.

Years later, after a three-week revival in Pastor Bresee's First Methodist Episcopal Church in Los Angeles, another unusual visitation of the Holy Spirit came to him. Evangelists MacDonald and Watson had conducted a series of revival services in his church. Soon afterward, while sitting in the parsonage, Pastor Bresee reported, "At this time there came to me in answer to prayer a very striking experience. I had been for some time in almost constant prayer, and crying to God for something that would meet my needs, not clearly realizing what they were, or how they could be met.

"I sat alone in the parsonage, in the cool of evening, in the front parlor near the door. The door being opened, I looked up into the azure in earnest prayer, while the shades of evening gathered about.

"As I waited and waited, and continued in prayer, looking up, it seemed to me as if from the azure there came a meteor, an indescribable ball of condensed light, descending rapidly toward me. As I gazed upon it, it was soon within a few score feet, when I seemed distinctly to hear a voice saying as my face was upturned toward it: 'Swallow it; swallow it,' and in an instant it fell upon my lips and face.

"I attempted to obey the injunction. It seemed to me, however, that I swallowed only a little of it, although it felt like fire on my lips, and the burning sensation did not leave for several days.

"While all of this of itself would be nothing, there came with it into my heart and being a transformed condition of life and blessing and unction and glory which I had never known before. I felt that my need was supplied.

"I have never gotten over it, and I have said very little relative to this; but there came into my ministry a new element of full salvation; there were more persons converted, and the last year of my ministry in that church was more consecutively successful, being crowned by an almost constant revival. When the third year came to a close, the church had been nearly doubled in membership, and in every way built up."

Pastor Bresee's enthusiastic emphasis upon entire sanctification irritated some of the bishops in the Methodist church. Frequently they called the second blessing "cranktification" and were apt to dub anyone who preached sanctification as a second work of grace a "holiness crank."

Bresee, however, instead of being a crank was more like a self-starter ignited by the Holy Spirit. It would have been impossible for him *not* to preach Bible holiness.

Providentially an opportunity to help organize and conduct the Peniel Mission came. It was undenominational, with the main objective being to minister to the poor and downtrodden. Pastor Bresee seemed well suited for this service as he had already been tagged as being "the friend of every bum and scalawag in town."

Church services, Sunday school, prayer meetings, revivals—they had it all at Peniel Mission. It was well organized and blessed by the Holy Spirit.

Then while Pastor Bresee was in Nebraska to assist in a national camp meeting, he received word from the directors of the mission that his services there would be no longer needed.

Just why seems to be a mystery. But it is not difficult to see providential leading again. Surely God had another plan for His faithful servant.

This plan culminated in the birth of a new church— the Church of the Nazarene. Its date of birth was October 30, 1895, and the place a small one-story building at 317 South Main Street in Los Angeles. There were 82 charter members. Because of frequent manifestations of the Holy Spirit in their simple meeting place, it soon became known as "The Glory Barn."

The main purposes of the church were to minister to the poor, crusade for temperance, and to preach and teach the doctrine of entire sanctification.

Within a year church membership had grown to 350.

Nazarene churches were organized up and down the west coast, in the Midwest, and in the Southland. Then came the uniting of large groups of holiness churches which climaxed in the official formation of the Church of the Nazarene on a national scale in October, 1908. In all these moves, Dr. Bresee was the recognized leader.

Dr. Bresee desired that holiness people all over America would unite to preach, teach, and evangelize. Writing in the *Nazarene Messenger,* he named as essential "the Triune Godhead in unity embracing the deity of

Jesus Christ and the personality of the Holy Ghost; the provision in the atonement for both the new birth and entire sanctification by the Holy Spirit, to which He also witnesses; growth in grace . . . which are essential to holiness."

He believed that strife over nonessentials divides people, but that there must be unity in believing such an essential as "The blood of Jesus Christ cleanseth from all sin."

Phineas F. Bresee contributed much to the Church of the Nazarene as an organizer, pastor, evangelist, Christian educator, author, and publisher.

"Position is nothing; reputation little," he said. "True godliness is the only thing which has any value. . . . All human effort to awaken sinners is as ineffective as preaching in a graveyard. . . . Keep the glory down! The Nazarenes are roughriders in the holiness movement."

He also said, "Let the Church of the Nazarene be true to its commission; not with great and elegant buildings; but let it feed the hungry, clothe the naked, wipe the tears from the sorrowing, and gather jewels for His diadem."

In October, 1915, at the General Assembly in Kansas City, General Superintendent Bresee, already ill, told the people, "I'll try to tarry until the next General Assembly; but in case I do not, I'll wait for you at the Eastern Gate."

He did not tarry long. On November 13, 1915, he arrived at the Eastern Gate, rejoicing, waiting . . .